WELL, BIRBAL?

JAHANPANAH, WE COULD EASILY SPARE SOME WISDOM.

BUT IT'LL TAKE TIME — PERHAPS A FEW WEEKS.

I'M WILLING TO WAIT.

LATER —

WELL, BIRBAL. I HOPE YOU KNOW WHAT YOU'RE DOING. OUR PRESTIGE IS AT STAKE.

DON'T WORRY, JAHANPANAH. THE KING OF CEYLON SHALL HAVE HIS POTFUL OF WISDOM.

THAT EVENING, BIRBAL SENT FOR HIS ATTENDANT.

BRING ME A FEW CLAY POTS WITH NARROW NECKS.

THE ATTENDANT SOON CAME BACK WITH THE POTS.

AH! THERE YOU ARE! GOOD. FOLLOW ME TO THE PUMPKIN PATCH.

BIRBAL CLAPPED HIS HANDS—

THE NEXT MOMENT, HIS ATTENDANT WALKED SOLEMNLY IN, CARRYING A TRAY WITH A POT ON IT.

HERE YOU ARE. YOU MAY TAKE IT TO YOUR KING. BUT REMEMBER...

...OUR PRECIOUS POT MUST BE RETURNED EMPTY AND INTACT. AND...

...THE FRUIT OF WISDOM THAT IT CONTAINS, TO BE OF ANY VALUE, MUST BE REMOVED WITHOUT A SCRATCH!

THE EMPEROR'S TOUCH

MY SON HAD SERVED IN THE ROYAL ARMY FOR TWENTY YEARS. BUT NOW, HE IS DEAD AND WE HAVE NO ONE TO TURN TO!

OUR EMPEROR IS KIND AND GENEROUS. HE WILL HELP YOU. DO AS I SAY.

ONE DAY, AN OLD WOMAN AND HER WIDOWED DAUGHTER-IN-LAW CAME TO BIRBAL.

THE FOLLOWING DAY, AT COURT—

JAHANPANAH, THIS SWORD ONCE WIELDED BY MY SON HAS WON MANY BATTLES FOR YOU. SO, PLEASE KEEP IT IN THE ARMOURY.

LET ME SEE IT.

THE SWORD WAS HANDED OVER TO THE EMPEROR. HE EXAMINED IT CAREFULLY.

IT'S OLD AND RUSTY... OF NO USE TO US WHATSOEVER.

8

WHY, BIRBAL, WHAT'S WRONG?

NOTHING, JAHAN-PANAH. IT'S ONLY THAT... I WAS CONFIDENT THE SWORD WOULD HAVE TURNED GOLDEN.

TURNED GOLDEN?

YES, JAHANPANAH. WHEN EVEN THE PARAS*, A MERE STONE, CAN TRANSMUTE IRON INTO GOLD...

...I'M SURPRISED THAT WHILE PASSING THROUGH YOUR BENEVOLENT HANDS...

...WELL...

AKBAR UNDERSTOOD.

GIVE THE WOMAN GOLD EQUAL TO THE WEIGHT OF THE SWORD.

AFTER RECEIVING THE GOLD, THE WOMEN WENT AWAY BLESSING THE EMPEROR —AND BIRBAL!

* A LEGENDARY STONE CREDITED WITH THE POWER OF CHANGING IRON INTO GOLD

A WIDOW'S SAVINGS

THE RICH AND THE POOR, THE YOUNG AND THE OLD, ALL SOUGHT BIRBAL'S HELP WHEN THEY WERE WRONGED. ONE DAY AN OLD WIDOW CAME TO SEE HIM.

HELP ME, HUZUR. I'VE BEEN SWINDLED.

BY WHOM?

IT'S A LONG STORY, HUZUR. SIX MONTHS AGO, I DECIDED TO GO ON A PILGRIMAGE.

BUT I WAS WORRIED ABOUT MY MONEY. I DIDN'T KNOW WHERE TO KEEP IT.

"FINALLY, I WENT TO A MENDICANT."

HERE IS A BAG OF COPPER COINS — ALL THAT I HAVE IN THIS WORLD. PLEASE KEEP IT FOR ME. IT WILL BE SAFE WITH YOU!

I'M SORRY. I CAN'T BE INVOLVED IN WORLDLY MATTERS. I DON'T TOUCH MONEY BUT...
...YOU MAY DIG A HOLE SOMEWHERE IN MY HUT AND BURY THE BAG THERE YOURSELF.
"SO I WENT TO A CORNER OF THE HUT AND DUG A SMALL HOLE."
MY COINS WILL BE SAFE HERE.
"ON MY RETURN, WHEN I WENT TO THE MENDICANT TO COLLECT THE MONEY —"
WHAT MONEY ARE YOU TALKING ABOUT ?
THE BAG OF COINS I BURIED IN YOUR HUT.

BUT SIR, I DID BURY IT HERE... THREE MONTHS AGO... IN **YOUR** PRESENCE!

QUITE POSSIBLE. BUT I AM BLIND TO WHAT GOES ON IN THIS MATERIALISTIC WORLD.

MY MIND HAS ONLY ONE THOUGHT—RAMA; MY EARS HEAR ONLY ONE SOUND—RAMA; MY EYES BEHOLD BUT ONE FORM— RAMA!

I CAME AWAY. WHAT ELSE *COULD* I DO?

COULD THE MENDICANT HAVE STOLEN YOUR COINS?

I AM SURE HE HAS. BUT I HAVE NO PROOF.

HM.

BIRBAL WENT INTO THE HUT AND FELL PROSTRATE IN FRONT OF THE MENDICANT.

BLESS ME, MASTER.

MAY YOU LIVE LONG, MY CHILD.

I HAVE HEARD PEOPLE TALK ABOUT YOUR SPIRITUAL EMINENCE. TODAY I HAVE HAD THE GOOD FORTUNE OF RECEIVING YOUR BLESSINGS.

I WONDER WHAT HE HAS IN THE CASKET. GOLD? JEWELS?

HOLY ONE, I HATE TO TROUBLE YOU WITH THE PROBLEMS WE FOOLISH MORTALS HAVE. BUT...

SPEAK UP, CHILD. LET ME HELP YOU IF I CAN.

NO, SIR. YOU MUSTN'T. YOU ARE A MAN OF GOD. I SHOULDN'T BURDEN YOU WITH WORLDLY WORRIES.

WHAT! IS HE GOING AWAY WITH THE CASKET?

BUT... BUT WHO ELSE CAN I TRUST IN THIS WICKED, WICKED WORLD? PLEASE GUIDE ME.

HE IS WAVERING. I MUST LAY HANDS ON THAT CASKET.

YOU MUST HAVE FORGOTTEN THE EXACT SPOT. WHY DON'T YOU LOOK FOR IT IN THAT CORNER?

THE WOMAN DID AS SHE WAS TOLD.

LATER —

YOU WERE RIGHT, O HOLY ONE! IT WAS IN THAT CORNER!

FOOLISH WOMAN! KEEPS HER MONEY IN ONE PLACE AND LOOKS FOR IT IN ANOTHER!

MONEY CAUSES WORRY. WORRY WEAKENS YOUR MEMORY. AND YOU LOSE YOUR BALANCE. WOULD YOU BELIEVE IT? THIS WOMAN EVEN ACCUSED ME OF STEALING HER MONEY!

amar chitra katha

Panel 1:
SO CHILD, BURY YOUR CASKET ANYWHERE BUT DO REMEMBER THE PLACE. I DON'T UNDERSTAND ANYTHING ABOUT THESE WORLDLY MATTERS.

I CAN SEE THAT!

Panel 2:
JUST THEN AN ATTENDANT CAME TO BIRBAL.

HUZUR, YOUR BROTHER HAS COME TO VISIT YOU! HE WANTS TO MEET YOU IMMEDIATELY.

OH, OH! SO I DON'T HAVE TO GO TO AJMER AFTER ALL!

Panel 3:
MAY I THANK YOU FOR YOUR KINDNESS, HOLY ONE?

Panel 4:
AND BIRBAL WALKED OUT WITH THE CASKET.

THE PERFECT PORTRAIT

ONE DAY, BIRBAL WAS SURPRISED TO FIND THE NORMALLY CHEERFUL COURT ARTIST LOOKING GLUM.

WHAT'S THE MATTER, MY FRIEND?

MY REPUTATION IS AT STAKE.

BUT YOU ARE THE BEST ARTIST THE COURT HAS EVER KNOWN. I DON'T UNDERSTAND...

YOU WILL, WHEN I'VE TOLD YOU THE WHOLE STORY.

THE ARTIST TOOK BIRBAL TO HIS HOUSE AND SHOWED HIM FIVE PORTRAITS.

THEY ARE OF A RICH NOBLE.

AREN'T THESE OF THE SAME MAN?

"A MONTH AGO HE THREW ME A CHALLENGE."

I BET, YOU CAN'T CREATE AN EXACT LIKENESS OF ME.

I BET, I CAN.

"HE POSED AND I GOT DOWN TO WORK. AT LAST —"

THAT'S ALL. I'LL GIVE THE PORTRAIT A FEW FINISHING TOUCHES AND BRING IT TO YOU TOMORROW.

"ON THE FOLLOWING DAY, WHEN I HANDED THE PORTRAIT TO HIM, CONFIDENT OF WINNING THE BET —"

THIS WON'T DO! IT ISN'T AN EXACT LIKENESS. I DON'T HAVE A BEARD!

BUT YOU DID HAVE ONE WHEN YOU POSED FOR THE PORTRAIT!

A BET IS A BET! AND AN EXACT LIKENESS AN EXACT LIKENESS! HERE! YOU MAY KEEP THIS AS A MEMENTO.

PLEASE GIVE ME ANOTHER CHANCE.

ALL RIGHT. YOU MAY TRY AGAIN.

SPEAK THE TRUTH BUT MAKE IT PLEASANT

THERE HE IS! AT IT AGAIN!

IF BIRBAL'S NEIGHBOUR HAD A WEAKNESS, IT WAS TO HAVE HIS FORTUNE TOLD.

SUDDENLY —

YOU FRAUD! DON'T YOU DARE COME THIS WAY AGAIN!

I WON'T! EVER!

BIRBAL WENT UP TO THE MAN.

WHAT DID YOU DO TO MAKE HIM SO ANGRY?

I READ HIS HOROSCOPE AND PREDICTED THAT HIS NEAR AND DEAR ONES WOULD DIE BEFORE HIM. AND THEN...

HE THREW YOU OUT, DIDN'T HE?

HE DID. HE COULDN'T FACE THE TRUTH, AND...

...I COULDN'T LIE.

YOU DID WELL TO SPEAK THE TRUTH BUT...

...YOU COULD HAVE MADE IT MORE PLEASANT!

PLEASANT? I DON'T UNDERSTAND. HOW...

IT'S SIMPLE. I'LL TELL YOU HOW. LISTEN...

...YOU'LL LIVE LONGER THAN ALL YOUR NEAR AND DEAR ONES!

REALLY? AND THAT RASCAL SAID YESTERDAY THAT...

NEVER MIND! WHY TALK OF INAUSPICIOUS MATTERS AT THIS AUSPICIOUS MOMENT? WAIT. I HAVE SOMETHING FOR YOU.

HE WENT IN AND CAME OUT WITH A BAG OF COINS.

DO COME AGAIN WHENEVER YOU HAVE THE TIME.

I WILL. MOST CERTAINLY!

LATER —

I NEVER DREAMT, HUZUR, THAT THE MANNER IN WHICH I WORD MY READING IS EVEN MORE IMPORTANT THAN THE READING ITSELF!

THE HOLY PARROT

ONE DAY, AKBAR'S FAVOURITE ATTENDANT CAME TO BIRBAL. HE WAS ALMOST IN TEARS.

HUZUR! HUZUR! YOU'VE GOT TO HELP ME! ONLY YOU CAN SAVE MY LIFE. I... THE EMPEROR...

YES... GO ON...

"A FEW MONTHS AGO, THE EMPEROR GAVE ME A PARROT."

IT'S A VERY SPECIAL BIRD; A HOLY MAN'S GIFT TO ME. TAKE GOOD CARE OF IT.

SHOULD ANYONE BRING ME NEWS OF ITS DEATH, I'LL BEHEAD HIM!

AND NOW... AND NOW IN SPITE OF MY LOVING CARE, IT SUDDENLY DIED. WHAT SHALL I DO?

IS THAT ALL? LEAVE IT TO ME. I'LL TAKE THE NEWS TO THE EMPEROR, AND YET SAVE MY HEAD!

LATER, AT AKBAR'S COURT —

JAHANPANAH, DO YOU REMEMBER THE PARROT THAT FAKIR GAVE YOU? IT'S A HOLY BIRD INDEED!

A HOLY BIRD, INDEED. HA! HA! HA!

IT IS, JAHANPANAH. I HAD GONE TO SEE IT. AND WHAT DO YOU THINK IT WAS DOING?

MEDITATING! WITH ITS EYES CLOSED AND ITS HEAD TURNED SKYWARDS!

YOU MUST BE JOKING.

SO THE TWO WENT TO THE ATTENDANT'S HOUSE. WHEN AKBAR SAW THE BIRD —

BIRBAL YOU MAY BE WISE, AND CLEVER! BUT THERE IS A LIMIT.

THIS BIRD IS DEAD! AND DON'T TELL ME YOU DIDN'T KNOW IT.

I DID. BUT I DIDN'T WANT TO BE BEHEADED!

ONLY THEN DID AKBAR REMEMBER WHAT HE HAD TOLD HIS ATTENDANT.

WELL! WELL! WELL! YOU'VE SAVED YET ANOTHER HEAD, BIRBAL. AND I'M GRATEFUL TO YOU FOR IT.

AKBAR THE HUNTER

AKBAR WAS EXTREMELY FOND OF HUNTING. ONE DAY—

HELP US, HUZOOR!

OUR VILLAGE IS BEING RAZED!

WHY ON EARTH?

THE KING WANTS MORE FORESTS IN HIS KINGDOM.

HIS MEN HAVE ORDERS TO CREATE MORE AND MORE NEW FORESTS.

THE KING WANTS NEW JUNGLES TO HUNT IN.

I'LL TRY AND DO WHAT I CAN.

ON THE NEXT HUNTING TRIP—

AH! THIS IS SO EXHILA-RATING. DON'T YOU THINK SO, BIRBAL?

UH, HUH!

LOOK AT THOSE OWLS!

CHI-CHI-THUP-THUP

THE TWO GROUPS SEEM TO BE HAVING A QUARREL.

BIRBAL IS SO WISE. HE SHOULD BE ABLE TO MAKE OUT WHAT THEY ARE SAYING.

YES, BIRBAL. TELL US WHY THEY ARE FIGHTING

I COULD TELL YOU BUT...

WHY DO YOU HESITATE?

YOUR MAJESTY MAY NOT LIKE TO HEAR IT.

GO ON. WHY SHOULD I MIND WHAT THE BIRDS SAY?

31

A GROUP OF OWLS HAVE COME FROM THE NEIGHBOURING KINGDOM TO MARRY ONE OF THEIR BOYS TO A GIRL OWL HERE.

THEY ARE ARRANGING FOR THE MARRIAGE. BUT THERE IS A DISPUTE BETWEEN THE GROOM'S FATHER AND THE BRIDE'S FATHER.

WHY?

THE BOY'S FATHER IS DEMANDING A GIFT OF FORTY FORESTS. BUT THE GIRL'S FATHER IS SAYING HE CANNOT COMPLY NOW...

... HOWEVER, AFTER A FEW YEARS, HE PROMISES TO GIFT EIGHTY FORESTS TO THE COUPLE.

HOW? IF HE DOESN'T HAVE FORTY FORESTS NOW, HOW WILL HE GIVE DOUBLE THE NUMBER LATER?

WELL, HE SAYS THE EMPEROR HERE IS VERY FOND OF HUNTING.

HE KEEPS CONVERTING VILLAGES INTO JUNGLES FOR HIS HUNTING PLEASURE SO THE NUMBER OF FORESTS IS SURE TO DOUBLE IN THE FUTURE.

AKBAR UNDERSTOOD THE MESSAGE BIRBAL WAS TRYING TO CONVEY.

YOU ARE RIGHT, BIRBAL. IT IS SELFISH OF ME TO DESTROY VILLAGE AFTER VILLAGE FOR MY HUNTING PLEASURE.

WHICH OF THE ACKS HAVE YOU STILL NOT READ?

ACK EPICS AND MYTHOLOGY

Best known stories from the Epics and the Puranas

ABHIMANYU
ANDHAKA
ANIRUDDHA
ARJUNA, TALES OF
ARUNI AND UTTANKA
ASHWINI KUMARS
AYYAPPAN
BAHUBALI
BALARAMA, TALES OF
BHEEMA AND HANUMAN
BHEESHMA
CHANDRAHASA
CHURNING OF THE OCEAN
DASHARATHA
DHRUVA AND ASHTAVAKRA
DRAUPADI
DRONA
DURGA, TALES OF
ELEPHANTA
GANDHARI
GANESHA
GANGA
GARUDA
GHATOTKACHA
GITA, THE
GOLDEN MONGOOSE, THE
HANUMAN
HANUMAN TO THE RESCUE
HARISCHANDRA
INDRA AND SHACHI
INDRA AND SHIBI
JAGANNATHA OF PURI
JAYADRATHA
KACHA AND DEVAYANI
KARNA
KARTTIKEYA
KRISHNA
KRISHNA AND JARASANDHA
KRISHNA AND NARAKASURA
KRISHNA AND RUKMINI
KRISHNA AND SHISHUPALA
KRISHNA AND THE FALSE
  VAASUDEVA
KUMBHAKARNA
LORD OF LANKA, THE
MAHABHARATA
MAHIRAVANA
NACHIKETA
NAHUSHA
NALA DAMAYANTI
NARADA, TALES OF
PANDAVA PRINCES, THE
PANDAVAS IN THE HIDING, THE
PRAHLAD
RAMA
RAVANA HUMBLED
SATI AND SHIVA
SAVITRI
SHIVA PARVATI
SHIVA, TALES OF
SONS OF RAMA, THE
SUDAMA
SURYA
SYAMANTAKA GEM, THE
TRIPURA
ULOOPI
UPANISHADS, TALES FROM
VALI
VISHNU, TALES OF
VISHWAMITRA

YAYATI
YUDHISHTHIRA, TALES OF

ACK INDIAN CLASSICS

Enchanting tales from Indian literature

ANANDA MATH
ANCESTORS OF RAMA
DEVI CHOUDHURANI
KANNAGI
KAPALA KUNDALA
MALAVIKA
RATNAVALI
SHAKUNTALA
UDAYANA
URVASHI
VASANTASENA
VASAVADATTA

ACK FABLES AND HUMOUR

Evergreen folktales, legends and tales of wisdom and humour

ACROBAT AND OTHER
  BUDDHIST TALES, THE
ADVENTURES OF
  AGAD DATTA, THE
ADVENTURES OF
  BADDU AND CHHOTU, THE
AMRAPALI
ANGULIMALA
BAG OF GOLD COINS, A
BATTLE OF WITS
BIKAL THE TERRIBLE
BIRBAL STORIES
  BIRBAL THE CLEVER
  BIRBAL THE GENIUS
  BIRBAL THE JUST
  BIRBAL THE WISE
  BIRBAL THE WITTY
  BIRBAL TO THE RESCUE
  THE INIMITABLE BIRBAL
CELESTIAL NECKLACE, THE
CHANDRALALAT
COWHERD OF ALAWI, THE
FEARLESS BOY AND OTHER
  BUDDHIST TALES, THE
FOOL'S DISCIPLES, THE
FRIENDS AND FOES
GOPAL AND THE COWHERD
GOPAL THE JESTER
HITOPADESHA TALES
  CHOICE OF FRIENDS
  HOW FRIENDS ARE PARTED
JATAKA TALES
  BIRD STORIES
  DEADLY FEAST, THE
  DEER STORIES
  ELEPHANT STORIES
  GIANT & THE DWARF, THE
  HIDDEN TREASURE, THE
  JACKAL STORIES
  MAGIC CHANT, THE
  MONKEY STORIES
  MOUSE MERCHANT, THE
  NANDIVISHALA
  STORIES OF COURAGE
  STORIES OF WISDOM
  TALES OF MISERS
  TRUE FRIENDS
KESARI THE FLYING THIEF
KING KUSHA
LEARNED PANDIT, THE

MAGIC GROVE, THE
MARYADA RAMA, TALES OF
PANCHATANTRA TALES
  BRAHMIN & THE GOAT
  CROWS AND OWLS
  DULLARD AND OTHER
    STORIES
  GREEDY MOTHER-IN-LAW, THE
  HOW THE JACKAL ATE THE
    ELEPHANT
  JACKAL &
    WAR DRUM, THE
  PRICELESS GEM, THE
  PRINCE AND THE
    MAGICIAN
  QUEEN'S NECKLACE, THE
PANDIT AND THE MILKMAID
RAMAN OF TENALI
RAMAN THE MATCHLESS WIT
SAKSHI GOPAL
SHRENIK
TIGER & THE WOODPECKER,
TIGER-EATER, THE
VIKRAMADITYA'S THRONE

ACK BRAVEHEARTS

Stirring tales of brave men and women of India

AJATASHATRU
AKBAR
AMAR SINGH RATHOR
ASHOKA
BAGHA JATIN
BAJI RAO I
BALADITYA & YASHODHARMA
BANDA BAHADUR
BAPPA RAWAL
BENI MADHO AND PIR ALI
BHAGAT SINGH
BIMBISARA
CHAND BIBI
CHANDRA SHEKHAR AZAD
CHANDRAGUPTA MAURYA
DURGADAS
ELLORA CAVES
HARSHA
HISTORIC CITY OF DELHI, THE
JAHANGIR
JALLIANWALA BAGH
KALPANA CHAWLA
KRISHNADEVA RAYA
KUNWAR SINGH
LACHIT BARPHUKAN
LALITADITYA
MANGAL PANDE
NOOR JAHAN
PADMINI
PANNA AND HADI RANI
PAURAVA AND ALEXANDER
PRITHVIRAJ CHAUHAN
RAJA BHOJA
RAJA RAJA CHOLA
RANA KUMBHA
RANA PRATAP
RANA SANGA
RANI ABBAKKA
RANI DURGAVATI
RANI OF JHANSI
RANJIT SINGH
RASH BEHARI BOSE
SAMUDRA GUPTA
SEA ROUTE TO INDIA
SHAH JAHAN
SHALIVAHANA

SHER SHAH
SHIVAJI
SHIVAJI, TALES OF
SUBHAS CHANDRA BOSE
SULTANA RAZIA
TANAJI
THE RANI OF KITTUR
TIPU SULTAN
VEER HAMMIR
VEER SAVARKAR
VELU THAMPI
VIKRAMADITYA

ACK VISIONARIES

Inspiring tales of thinkers, social reformers and nation builders

ADI SHANKARA
AMBEDKAR, BABASAHEB
BASAVESHWARA
BIRLA G.D.
BUDDHA
CHANAKYA
CHAITANYA MAHAPRABHU
CHINMAYANANDA, SWAMI
CHOKHA MELA
DAYANANDA
DESHBANDHU
  CHITTANRANJAN DAS
FA HIEN
GURU ARJAN
GURU GOBIND SINGH
GURU NANAK
GURU TEGH BAHADUR
HIUEN TSANG
J.R.D.TATA
JAGADIS CHANDRA BOSE
JAMSETJI TATA
JAWAHARLAL NEHRU
JAYAPRAKASH NARAYAN
JNANESHWAR
KABIR
KALIDASA
LAL BAHADUR SHASTRI
LOKAMANYA TILAK
MADHVACHARYA
MAHAVIRA
MEGASTHENES
MIRABAI
MOTHER TERESA
PRANAVANANDA, SWAMI
RABINDRANATH TAGORE
RAMAKRISHNA, SRI
RAMANA MAHARSHI
RAMANUJA
RAM SHASTRI
SAIBABA, TALES OF
SHANKAR DEV
SOORDAS
SUBRAMANIA BHARATI
TANSEN
TULSIDAS
VIDYASAGAR
VIVEKANANDA
ZARATHUSHTRA

ACK SPECIAL ISSUES

BHAGAWAT - THE KRISHNA AVATAR
DASHA AVATAR
JESUS CHRIST
MAHABHARATA
MAHATMA GANDHI
RAM CHARIT MANAS
VALMIKI'S RAMAYANA

 All titles available on www.AmarChitraKatha.com

BIRBAL TO THE RESCUE

Pity the thief or hypocrite who crosses Birbal's path. The poor man will be either hopelessly embarrassed or pleased to escape with his life. With an unfailing eye for human weakness, Birbal protects the innocent. People, from every strata of society, flock to him for help with endless lists of woes. Known for his compassion and tact, Birbal never fails them, even if it means pitting his wits against the all-powerful Emperor.

OTHER ACK FABLES & HUMOUR:

BIRBAL THE JUST

BIRBAL THE WISE

THE DULLARD

THE GREEDY MOTHER-IN-LAW

ALSO LOOK FOR:

GHATOTKACHA

MALAVIKA

BAJI RAO 1

TANSEN
THE MUSICAL GEM

EPICS & MYTHOLOGY

INDIAN CLASSICS

BRAVEHEARTS

VISIONARIES

T3-ATF-717

www.ack-me...

ISBN 81-8482

THE INIMITABLE BIRBAL

A FRIEND, PHILOSOPHER AND GUIDE TO AKBAR

Vol 580 | ₹50

The route to your roots

When they look back at their formative years, many Indians nostalgically recall the vital part Amar Chitra Katha picture books have played in their lives. It was **ACK – Amar Chitra Katha** – that first gave them a glimpse of their glorious heritage.

Since they were introduced in 1967, there are now **over 400 Amar Chitra Katha** titles to choose from. **Over 90 million copies** have been sold worldwide.

Now the Amar Chitra Katha titles are even more widely available in **1000+ bookstores all across India**. Log on to www.ack-media.com to locate a bookstore near you. If you do not have access to a bookstore, you can buy all the titles through our online store **www.amarchitrakatha.com**. We provide quick delivery anywhere in the world.

To make it easy for you to locate the titles of your choice from our treasure trove of titles, the books are now arranged in five categories.

Epics and Mythology
Best known stories from the Epics and the Puranas

Indian Classics
Enchanting tales from Indian literature

Fables and Humour
Evergreen folktales, legends and tales of wisdom and humour

Bravehearts
Stirring tales of brave men and women of India

Visionaries
Inspiring tales of thinkers, social reformers and nation builders

Contemporary Classic
The Best of Modern Indian literature

Script	Illustrations	Editor
Margie Sastry	Ram Waeerkar	Anant Pai

Amar Chitra Katha Pvt Ltd

© Amar Chitra Katha Pvt Ltd, 1989, Reprinted October 2012, ISBN 978-81-8482-043-0
Published & Printed by Amar Chitra Katha Pvt. Ltd., Krishna House, 3rd Floor,
Raghuvanshi Mill Compound, S.B.Marg, Lower Parel (W), Mumbai- 400 013. India
For Consumer Complaints Contact Tel : +91-22 40497436
Email: customerservice@ack-media.com